Bright Kant

Fun Things to do in Retirement

Embrace the Golden Years | Exciting Adventures and Activities for Retirement Bliss .

Contents

1.

2.

3.

4.

5.

Foreword

Welcome to "Fun Things to Do in Retirement: Embrace the Golden Years." This book is your ultimate guide to unlocking the full potential of your retirement and creating a fulfilling and exciting chapter in your life. Retirement is a time to cherish, a phase where you have the freedom to explore new horizons, indulge in your passions, and savor the joys of leisurely pursuits.

In these pages, you will discover an extensive collection of 101 exciting adventures and activities that are sure to ignite your imagination, invigorate your spirit, and bring a renewed sense of purpose to your retirement years. Whether you are seeking thrilling experiences, creative outlets, social connections, or personal growth, this book has something for everyone.

From embarking on thrilling travel adventures to delving into captivating hobbies, from engaging in fulfilling volunteer work to discovering new talents, this guide covers a wide range of possibilities to suit every interest and personality. Each activity is carefully curated to provide a balance of enjoyment, enrichment, and rejuvenation, ensuring that your retirement is nothing short of extraordinary.

With practical tips, inspiring anecdotes, and helpful resources, this book will empower you to make the most of your retirement, allowing you to embrace the golden years with enthusiasm, vitality, and a zest for life. Whether you are newly retired or have been enjoying this phase for a while, "Fun Things to Do in Retirement: Embrace the Golden Years" will be your trusted companion as you embark on this remarkable journey of self-discovery, adventure, and pure joy.

So, get ready to embark on a remarkable voyage of exploration, growth, and fulfillment. Let the pages of this book be your gateway to a retirement filled with laughter, discovery, and endless possibilities. Embrace the golden years and embark on exciting adventures and activities for retirement bliss!

1

1-10 Fun Things to do in Retirement

1. Travel to your dream destinations: Traveling to your dream destinations is a thrilling and enriching experience that can be a highlight of your retirement years. After years of hard work and dedication, retirement offers the perfect opportunity to fulfill your travel aspirations and explore the world in ways you've always dreamed of. Whether you yearn for bustling cities, serene natural landscapes, cultural immersion, or historical wonders, there are endless possibilities awaiting you.

One of the greatest benefits of retirement travel is the flexibility it offers. You can now plan trips without worrying about work schedules or limited vacation days. You have the freedom to choose the timing that suits you best, whether it's avoiding peak tourist seasons or taking advantage of off-peak rates and quieter surroundings.

Retirement allows you to travel at a more relaxed pace, savoring every moment and fully immersing yourself in the destinations you visit. You can take the time to connect with the local culture, indulge in authentic cuisine, and engage in meaningful interactions with locals. Traveling in retirement opens doors to unique experiences that may not have been feasible during your working years.

To make the most of your retirement travels, it's important to plan ahead and consider your personal preferences and interests. Reflect on the destinations that have always captured your imagination and start creating a bucket list of must-visit places. Research different aspects of your dream destinations, such as the local customs, historical landmarks, natural wonders, and iconic attractions.

Consider the type of travel experiences you desire. Are you interested in exploring ancient ruins, lounging on picturesque beaches, embarking on adventurous hikes, or immersing yourself in vibrant city life? Tailor your travel plans to include a mix of activities that align with your passions and interests.

When it comes to logistics, retirement offers the opportunity for more flexibility and spontaneity. You can choose to embark on extended trips to fully immerse yourself in a particular region or take shorter, more frequent getaways. Consider different modes of travel, such as cruises, road trips, or train journeys, to add variety and a sense of adventure to your retirement travels.

While it's important to be open to new experiences, don't forget to prioritize your comfort and well-being. Choose accommodations that cater to your needs and preferences, whether it's luxury resorts, cozy bed and breakfasts, or immersive homestays. Take into account any physical limitations or health considerations when planning activities and destinations, ensuring that your travel experiences are enjoyable and stress-free.

Finally, embrace the joy of sharing your travel adventures with loved ones. Whether it's traveling with your spouse, friends, or joining group tours, creating shared memories can enhance the overall experience and deepen your connections.

Traveling to your dream destinations in retirement is a remarkable opportunity to broaden your horizons, expand your cultural understanding, and create lifelong memories. Embrace the freedom and flexibility that retirement brings, and let your wanderlust guide you to the places you've always longed to explore. Whether it's stepping foot on a remote island, wandering through ancient ruins, or getting lost in the vibrant streets of a bustling city, retirement travel can be an exhilarating journey of discovery and fulfillment.

2. **Take up a new hobby, like painting, gardening, or cooking:** Taking up a new hobby in retirement can be a fulfilling and enriching way to explore your passions, cultivate new skills, and engage in activities that bring you joy. Whether it's painting, gardening, cooking, or any other creative pursuit, hobbies offer a multitude of benefits that contribute to a vibrant and fulfilling retirement.

One popular hobby that many retirees embrace is painting. Painting allows for self-expression, creativity, and the opportunity to explore different artistic styles and techniques. Whether you choose to work with acrylics, watercolors, oils, or other mediums, painting provides a therapeutic outlet that can reduce stress and enhance overall well-being. It's a hobby that encourages personal growth, as you develop your artistic skills and create meaningful pieces of art that reflect your unique perspective.

Gardening is another hobby that holds immense appeal for retirees. It allows you to connect with nature, nurture plant life, and create beautiful outdoor spaces. Whether you have a small balcony or a spacious backyard, gardening offers endless possibilities. You can grow your own vegetables and herbs, cultivate a vibrant flower garden, or even experiment with bonsai or indoor plants. Gardening provides a sense of accomplishment as you witness the growth and transformation of your plants, and it also offers physical activity and a connection to the natural world.

Cooking is a hobby that can be both enjoyable and delicious. Retirement provides the perfect opportunity to expand your culinary skills and experiment with new recipes and flavors. Whether you've always wanted to master a specific cuisine or simply enjoy cooking for family and friends, exploring the culinary arts can be a rewarding endeavor. You can take cooking classes, join cooking clubs or online communities, and even host dinner parties to showcase your culinary creations. Cooking not only satisfies your taste buds but also allows you to nourish yourself and others with delicious meals made with love.

Engaging in hobbies like painting, gardening, and cooking offers more than just the activity itself. It provides a sense of purpose, fulfillment, and personal growth. Hobbies can also foster social connections and create opportunities for you to connect with others who share similar interests. Joining painting groups, gardening clubs, or cooking classes can introduce you to like-minded individuals and expand your social circle, fostering a sense of camaraderie and community.

Furthermore, hobbies can be flexible and adaptable to suit your preferences and lifestyle. You can devote as much or as little time as you desire, allowing you to strike a balance between pursuing your hobbies and engaging in other activities or commitments. Hobbies in retirement provide an avenue for continuous learning, exploration, and personal fulfillment, allowing you to tap into your passions and develop new skills throughout your retirement years.

In conclusion, taking up a new hobby like painting, gardening, or cooking can add immense value and joy to your retirement. These hobbies provide avenues for self-expression, creativity, personal growth, and social connections. They allow you to explore your interests, learn new skills, and find fulfillment in pursuing activities that bring you happiness. So, whether you pick up a paintbrush, put on gardening gloves, or grab a chef's apron, embracing a new hobby in retirement is an opportunity to ignite your passion and make the most of this exciting chapter in your life.

3. Start a book club with fellow retirees: Starting a book club with fellow retirees can be an enriching and rewarding experience that fosters intellectual stimulation, social connection, and a love for literature. It provides a platform for retirees to come together, share their perspectives, and engage in meaningful discussions about books and ideas. Whether you are an avid reader or someone looking to explore the world of literature, a book club can offer a range of benefits during your retirement years.

One of the primary advantages of starting a book club in retirement is the opportunity for intellectual engagement. Reading and discussing books opens up new horizons, exposes you to different genres, and encourages critical thinking. The book club setting allows you to explore diverse topics, authors, and writing styles that you may not have encountered on your own. It's a chance to broaden your literary knowledge and deepen your understanding of various subjects.

A book club also creates a social space for retirees to connect and build friendships with like-minded individuals. Sharing a love for literature brings people together, fostering a sense of camaraderie and camaraderie. Book club meetings offer a platform for meaningful conversations and the exchange of ideas, enhancing social connections and providing a sense of belonging. It's an opportunity to form lasting bonds with fellow retirees who share your passion for books.

The structure of a book club allows for regular meetings and discussions, providing a sense of routine and purpose in retirement. It gives you a reason to look forward to engaging conversations and the motivation to keep reading. As each member brings their unique perspectives and interpretations to the table, book club discussions can be intellectually stimulating, thought-provoking, and even transformative.

Starting a book club in retirement also encourages lifelong learning and personal growth. It prompts you to read outside your comfort zone, explore different genres, and delve into literary works that challenge and inspire you. The discussions allow you to gain new insights, develop critical thinking skills, and expand your understanding of the world. It's a journey of continuous learning and self-discovery that keeps your mind sharp and engaged.

When starting a book club, you have the freedom to shape it according to your preferences. You can choose a specific genre, focus on classic literature, or have a theme for each month. You can decide on the frequency and location of meetings, whether it's in-person gatherings or online discussions. Additionally, with the availability of digital platforms and online forums, book clubs can connect retirees from different locations, making it accessible and inclusive.

In conclusion, starting a book club with fellow retirees is an excellent way to engage intellectually, foster social connections, and explore the world of literature. It offers a platform for vibrant discussions, lifelong learning, and the joy of shared reading experiences. Whether you are starting a club with existing friends or reaching out to new acquaintances, a book club in retirement opens the door to new perspectives, meaningful conversations, and lasting friendships. So gather your favorite books, invite fellow retirees, and embark on a literary journey that will enrich your retirement years in countless ways.

4. Volunteer for a cause you're passionate about: Volunteering for a cause you're passionate about is a deeply fulfilling and purposeful way to spend your retirement years. It allows you to contribute your time, skills, and experience to make a positive impact in the lives of others and the community. Volunteering not only benefits those in need but also brings numerous rewards and personal satisfaction to the volunteers themselves.

One of the key benefits of volunteering in retirement is the opportunity to pursue a cause that holds special meaning to you. Whether it's supporting education, promoting environmental sustainability, assisting in healthcare, advocating for social justice, or working with animals, there are countless causes to choose from. By aligning your volunteer efforts with your passions, you can channel your energy and expertise into areas that resonate deeply with your values and personal interests.

Volunteering offers a chance to utilize and share the skills and knowledge you've acquired throughout your life. Your professional expertise and life experiences can be invaluable assets to organizations and communities in need. Whether it's mentoring young professionals, providing guidance to nonprofit organizations, or offering specialized services, your skills and wisdom can make a significant difference in the lives of others. Volunteering allows you to leave a lasting legacy and contribute to positive change in the world.

Engaging in volunteer work in retirement also presents opportunities for personal growth and learning. You may encounter new challenges, expand your horizons, and develop new skills as you adapt to different environments and circumstances. Volunteering exposes you to diverse perspectives, cultures, and experiences, fostering empathy, understanding, and a broader worldview.

Another significant aspect of volunteering is the social connection and sense of community it provides. It allows you to meet like-minded individuals who share your passion for the cause. Building relationships with fellow volunteers, staff members, and the individuals you serve can lead to lifelong friendships and a strong support network. Volunteering in retirement offers a chance to connect with people of different backgrounds and generations, bridging gaps and creating a sense of belonging.

Volunteering can also have positive effects on your overall well-being. Numerous studies have shown that volunteering is associated with improved mental and physical health. It can reduce stress, combat feelings of loneliness and isolation, and provide a sense of purpose and fulfillment. The act of giving back and making a difference in the lives of others can bring a deep sense of joy and satisfaction.

When considering volunteering in retirement, it's important to find opportunities that fit your interests, availability, and capabilities. Research local organizations, community centers, and nonprofit groups that align with your chosen cause. Reach out to them to learn about their volunteer programs and how you can contribute. Consider both short-term and long-term commitments, as well as the flexibility to accommodate your other retirement activities and responsibilities.

In conclusion, volunteering for a cause you're passionate about in retirement is a meaningful and rewarding endeavor. It provides an opportunity to make a positive impact, utilize your skills and experiences, and foster personal growth. Whether it's dedicating your time to a local charity, mentoring individuals, or advocating for a cause you believe in, volunteering offers a chance to leave a lasting legacy and contribute to a better world. Embrace the power of giving back and discover the profound joy that comes from making a difference in the lives of others.

5. Learn a musical instrument: Learning a musical instrument in retirement can be a fulfilling and enriching endeavor that brings joy, creativity, and a sense of accomplishment. Whether you've always had a passion for music or are looking to explore a new artistic avenue, playing a musical instrument offers a range of benefits that can enhance your retirement experience.

One of the primary advantages of learning a musical instrument in retirement is the opportunity for personal expression and creativity. Playing an instrument allows you to tap into your artistic side, expressing emotions and ideas through the power of music. It provides a means to explore different genres, styles, and techniques, enabling you to develop your own unique musical voice.

Learning a musical instrument also stimulates cognitive function and mental acuity. It requires focus, concentration, and coordination, which can help keep your mind sharp and agile. As you navigate melodies, rhythms, and chords, you are actively exercising your brain, fostering memory retention, and enhancing problem-solving skills. This mental engagement can have positive effects on overall brain health and cognitive abilities.

Playing a musical instrument can be a deeply rewarding and enjoyable experience. It allows you to immerse yourself in the beauty of music, creating melodies and harmonies that resonate with your soul. Whether you choose a piano, guitar, violin, flute, or any other instrument, the act of playing can provide a sense of tranquility, stress relief, and emotional well-being. It offers a way to express yourself and find solace in the melodies you create.

Learning a musical instrument also opens doors to new social connections and opportunities for collaboration. You can seek out local music groups, bands, or orchestras to join and engage with fellow musicians. Playing in an ensemble or participating in jam sessions allows you to connect with like-minded individuals, share your passion for music, and create beautiful harmonies together. These social interactions can foster a sense of camaraderie and belonging, enhancing your retirement experience.

Moreover, the flexibility and adaptability of learning a musical instrument make it suitable for retirement. You can tailor your practice schedule to fit your availability and desired level of commitment. Whether you prefer to take formal lessons, learn through online tutorials, or explore self-guided learning, there are numerous resources available to support your musical journey. The process of learning and improving your skills can provide a sense of accomplishment and personal growth.

It's important to approach learning a musical instrument in retirement with patience and a growth mindset. Embrace the journey of acquiring new skills and enjoy the process of improvement. Set realistic goals, celebrate milestones, and allow yourself the freedom to make mistakes and learn from them. Remember that the true value lies in the joy of playing and the personal satisfaction it brings.

In conclusion, learning a musical instrument in retirement offers a wealth of benefits and opportunities for personal growth. It provides a means for self-expression, enhances cognitive function, and brings a sense of fulfillment and joy. Whether you are starting from scratch or revisiting an instrument you played in the past, the experience of learning and playing music can be a lifelong pursuit that enriches your retirement years. So, embrace the melody, explore the rhythms, and embark on a musical journey that will bring harmony to your retirement days.

6. Join a dance or fitness class: Joining a dance or fitness class in retirement can be an invigorating and enjoyable way to stay active, maintain physical fitness, and engage with a vibrant community of like-minded individuals. Dance and fitness classes offer a range of benefits that contribute to overall well-being and a fulfilling retirement experience.

Participating in dance or fitness classes provides an avenue for regular physical exercise, which is essential for maintaining good health in retirement. Engaging in regular physical activity can help improve cardiovascular health, increase strength and flexibility, enhance balance and coordination, and boost overall energy levels. Dance classes, in particular, offer a fun and dynamic way to stay active, combining movement with music and rhythm.

Joining a dance or fitness class also offers opportunities for social connection and community engagement. These classes often bring together individuals of various ages and backgrounds who share a common interest in movement and wellness. By participating in group activities, you can form new friendships, build a support network, and develop a sense of camaraderie with your fellow classmates. The social interactions and shared experiences can add an extra layer of enjoyment to your retirement journey.

Dance classes provide an artistic outlet for self-expression and creativity. Through various dance styles like ballet, jazz, hip-hop, salsa, or ballroom, you can explore different movements, learn choreography, and express emotions through body language. Dance allows you to tap into your artistic side, igniting a sense of joy and liberation as you move to the rhythm of the music.

Fitness classes, on the other hand, offer a diverse range of exercise options to cater to different preferences and fitness levels. Whether it's yoga, Pilates, Zumba, aerobics, strength training, or aquatic exercises, fitness classes provide an opportunity to improve physical fitness, increase flexibility, and boost overall well-being. These classes are often designed to be accessible and adaptable, allowing individuals of all ages and fitness levels to participate and progress at their own pace.

By joining a dance or fitness class, you can also benefit from expert guidance and instruction from qualified instructors. These professionals can provide proper technique guidance, offer modifications for individual needs, and ensure a safe and effective workout. Their expertise can help you maximize the benefits of each class and progress in your fitness or dance journey.

Participating in dance or fitness classes also offers a structured routine and a sense of purpose in retirement. Having regular class schedules and commitments can help you stay motivated and dedicated to your fitness goals. It provides a sense of achievement as you make progress, learn new skills, and see improvements in your physical abilities over time.

Lastly, dance and fitness classes are inclusive and welcoming environments that promote body positivity and self-acceptance. They encourage participants to focus on their own progress and well-being rather than comparisons or societal expectations. Engaging in these activities can boost self-confidence, enhance body awareness, and foster a positive relationship with your body, regardless of age or physical abilities.

In conclusion, joining a dance or fitness class in retirement offers a multitude of benefits for physical, social, and emotional well-being. These classes provide opportunities for regular exercise, artistic expression, social connection, and personal growth. By engaging in these activities, you can maintain an active lifestyle, improve fitness levels, and enjoy the numerous joys that come with dancing and staying physically fit in retirement. So, put on your dancing shoes or workout gear, embrace the rhythm, and step into a world of movement, wellness, and fulfillment.

7. Take up photography and capture beautiful moments: Taking up photography as a hobby in retirement can be a fulfilling and creative pursuit that allows you to capture and preserve beautiful moments in your life and the world around you. Photography provides a means to express yourself artistically, explore your surroundings with a new perspective, and create visual narratives that tell stories.

One of the main benefits of photography is the ability to capture and freeze fleeting moments in time. With a camera in hand, you can document special occasions, significant milestones, and everyday moments that hold personal meaning. Photography allows you to create a visual diary of your retirement journey, capturing memories and experiences that can be cherished for years to come.

Engaging in photography also encourages mindfulness and a deeper appreciation for the present moment. As you search for interesting subjects and compose your shots, you become more attuned to the details and beauty in your surroundings. Photography provides an opportunity to slow down, observe, and truly connect with the world. It allows you to find beauty in the simplest of things and encourages a sense of gratitude for the wonders that surround us.

Photography is a versatile art form that allows for personal expression and creativity. With different techniques, perspectives, and editing styles, you can develop your own unique photographic style. Whether you're drawn to landscapes, portraits, still life, street photography, or any other genre, photography offers a canvas for self-expression and experimentation. It allows you to convey emotions, capture the essence of a moment, and share your unique perspective with others.

Taking up photography in retirement also presents opportunities for continuous learning and personal growth. The world of photography is vast and ever-evolving, with new technologies, techniques, and trends emerging constantly. You can expand your technical skills, explore different genres, and learn from the work of other photographers. Engaging in photography communities, workshops, or online forums can offer valuable insights, feedback, and inspiration to fuel your growth as a photographer.

Photography also encourages exploration and discovery. As you embark on photographic adventures, you may find yourself venturing into new places, seeking out interesting subjects, and immersing yourself in different cultures or natural landscapes. Photography can be a catalyst for exploration, pushing you to go beyond your comfort zone and discover hidden gems in your local area or during your travels.

Furthermore, photography provides opportunities for sharing and connecting with others. You can showcase your work through exhibitions, social media platforms, or even by creating photo albums for family and friends. Sharing your photographs allows you to evoke emotions, spark conversations, and create connections with others who appreciate and resonate with your images. It can be a way to inspire, entertain, and leave a lasting impact on others.

In conclusion, taking up photography in retirement offers a plethora of benefits and opportunities for self-expression, creativity, and personal growth. It allows you to capture and preserve moments, explore the world with a new perspective, and create visual stories that reflect your unique vision. Photography invites you to be present, appreciate the beauty around you, and share your experiences with others. So, grab your camera, embrace the world as your canvas, and embark on a journey of capturing beautiful moments that will become a treasure trove of memories in your retirement years.

8. Learn a new language: Learning a new language in retirement can be an exciting and rewarding pursuit that opens doors to new cultures, enhances cognitive abilities, and provides opportunities for personal growth and connection. Whether you want to travel, communicate with family and friends, or simply challenge yourself intellectually, learning a new language offers a range of benefits that can enrich your retirement experience.

One of the primary advantages of learning a new language is the ability to connect with different cultures and communities. Language is a powerful tool that allows you to bridge communication gaps, gain insight into different perspectives, and develop a deeper understanding of diverse cultures. By learning a new language, you gain access to a wealth of literature, music, films, and traditions that can broaden your horizons and foster a sense of global citizenship.

Learning a new language also exercises and enhances cognitive function. Research has shown that language learning can improve memory, enhance problem-solving skills, and sharpen overall cognitive abilities. It challenges your brain to think in new ways, making connections between words and concepts, and improving your mental agility. These cognitive benefits contribute to maintaining mental sharpness and promoting healthy brain aging.

Engaging in language learning in retirement offers a sense of purpose and intellectual stimulation. It provides a new challenge and a goal to work towards, igniting a sense of curiosity and motivation. As you progress in your language studies, you experience a sense of accomplishment and personal growth, boosting self-confidence and self-esteem. Language learning encourages a growth mindset, as you embrace the process of acquiring new skills and embrace the joys of language acquisition.

Learning a new language can also enhance travel experiences. When you travel to countries where the language is spoken, knowing the local language can greatly enrich your interactions and allow for a more immersive experience. It enables you to communicate with locals, navigate daily life more effectively, and gain deeper insights into the culture and customs of the places you visit. Speaking the local language can open doors to meaningful connections and create unforgettable experiences.

Additionally, learning a new language can promote social connections and foster new friendships. Joining language exchange programs, conversation groups, or language classes introduces you to a community of fellow language learners and native speakers. Engaging in language practice and cultural exchanges provides opportunities to build relationships, share experiences, and develop connections with people from different backgrounds. Language learning can be a catalyst for creating lasting friendships and a sense of belonging.

Fortunately, in the digital age, there are numerous resources available for language learning. You can choose from online language courses, mobile apps, language exchange platforms, or in-person classes offered in your community. These resources provide interactive and engaging materials, audiovisual content, and opportunities for practice and feedback. It's important to find a learning method that suits your preferences and learning style, allowing you to progress at a pace that is comfortable for you.

In conclusion, learning a new language in retirement is a fulfilling and enriching pursuit that provides numerous benefits. It allows you to connect with different cultures, exercise your cognitive abilities, and foster personal growth. Whether you aspire to travel, communicate with others, or challenge yourself intellectually, language learning opens doors to new experiences, connections, and opportunities. So, seize the opportunity to embark on a linguistic adventure and embrace the joys of learning a new language in your retirement years.

9. Explore local museums and art galleries: Exploring local museums and art galleries in retirement offers a rich and fulfilling way to immerse yourself in culture, expand your knowledge, and appreciate the beauty of artistic expressions. Museums and art galleries provide a window into history, diverse perspectives, and the creativity of artists from different eras and regions. They offer a range of benefits that can enhance your retirement experience.

One of the primary advantages of exploring local museums and art galleries is the opportunity to engage with history and cultural heritage. Museums showcase artifacts, historical objects, and exhibitions that provide insights into the past, allowing you to connect with different time periods and civilizations. Art galleries, on the other hand, exhibit works of art that capture the essence of different periods, styles, and artistic movements. By exploring these cultural institutions, you can gain a deeper understanding of human history, artistic evolution, and cultural diversity.

Visiting museums and art galleries also promotes lifelong learning and intellectual stimulation. They provide a wealth of educational opportunities through guided tours, lectures, workshops, and interactive exhibits. As you engage with the displays, read descriptions, and listen to experts, you can broaden your knowledge, deepen your understanding, and challenge your perspectives. Museums and art galleries encourage curiosity and a thirst for learning, creating a platform for continuous personal growth.

Furthermore, exploring local museums and art galleries fosters an appreciation for the arts and nurtures creativity. By experiencing a diverse range of artistic expressions, you can develop a deeper understanding and admiration for different artistic styles, techniques, and interpretations. Viewing visual art can inspire and ignite your own creativity, encouraging you to pursue artistic hobbies, express yourself through various mediums, or even create your own works of art. Museums and art galleries can serve as a wellspring of inspiration and a catalyst for personal artistic exploration.

Visiting these cultural institutions can also provide a sense of tranquility, inspiration, and emotional well-being. Immersing yourself in the serene atmosphere of a museum or art gallery allows for reflection, introspection, and appreciation of the beauty around you. Art has the power to evoke emotions, tell stories, and evoke a sense of wonder. Taking the time to appreciate art can offer respite from daily stresses, promote mindfulness, and nurture your mental and emotional well-being.

Moreover, exploring local museums and art galleries offers opportunities for social engagement and community connection. You can visit these cultural institutions with family, friends, or join organized tours or groups that cater to fellow enthusiasts. Sharing the experience with others can spark conversations, foster connections, and deepen relationships. It provides a platform for shared interests, cultural dialogue, and the exchange of ideas.

In today's world, many museums and art galleries offer digital platforms and virtual tours, making art and culture more accessible than ever. Even if you cannot physically visit a museum or art gallery, you can explore their collections, exhibits, and educational resources online. Virtual experiences can provide a taste of the art world and inspire future visits.

In conclusion, exploring local museums and art galleries in retirement is an enriching and culturally immersive experience. It offers a chance to connect with history, nurture creativity, and appreciate the beauty of artistic expressions. Museums and art galleries promote lifelong learning, intellectual stimulation, and emotional well-being. So, embrace the opportunity to embark on artistic adventures, uncover hidden treasures, and immerse yourself in the wonders of art and culture during your retirement years.

10. Join a community theater group: Joining a community theater group in retirement can be a fulfilling and exciting way to explore your creativity, build social connections, and indulge in the joy of performing arts. Community theater offers a range of opportunities for individuals with a passion for acting, singing, dancing, or even behind-the-scenes work. It allows you to engage with a vibrant community of artists, create memorable experiences, and share your talents with others.

One of the primary advantages of joining a community theater group is the opportunity to unleash your creative potential. Theater provides a platform for self-expression, allowing you to step into different roles, explore emotions, and tell stories through the power of acting. Whether you are a seasoned performer or new to the stage, community theater welcomes individuals of all skill levels and encourages artistic growth and development. Through rehearsals, workshops, and performances, you can enhance your acting abilities, improve stage presence, and refine your craft.

Engaging in community theater also fosters a strong sense of camaraderie and social connection. By becoming a part of a theater group, you join a community of like-minded individuals who share a passion for the performing arts. You work together towards a common goal, supporting and collaborating with fellow actors, directors, designers, and crew members. Theater fosters a sense of teamwork, trust, and friendship as you navigate the creative process together. The bonds formed in the theater community can be deep and long-lasting, creating a network of support and belonging.

Joining a community theater group offers the opportunity to learn and acquire new skills. Beyond acting, theater provides a wealth of opportunities to explore other areas such as singing, dancing, stage management, set design, lighting, and more. You can participate in workshops, receive guidance from experienced professionals, and gain hands-on experience in various aspects of theater production. Community theater encourages continuous learning, growth, and a spirit of exploration.

Being a part of a theater production can also provide a sense of purpose and structure in retirement. It offers a regular schedule of rehearsals, performances, and events, giving you a sense of routine and something to look forward to. The demands of learning lines, practicing choreography, and preparing for shows can provide a healthy challenge and stimulate mental agility. Theater helps keep your mind sharp, boosts memory skills, and encourages continuous growth as you take on new roles and characters.

Moreover, community theater allows you to engage with and contribute to the local community. Performances and productions bring people together, creating shared experiences and entertainment for audiences of all ages. By participating in community theater, you help enrich the cultural fabric of your community, offering a source of inspiration, entertainment, and artistic expression. Theater has the power to evoke emotions, provoke thought, and create lasting memories for both performers and audiences.

In conclusion, joining a community theater group in retirement offers a wealth of benefits and opportunities for personal growth, social connection, and artistic expression. It provides a platform to unleash your creativity, learn new skills, and engage with a vibrant community of artists. Community theater encourages teamwork, camaraderie, and the joy of performing arts. So, step into the spotlight, embrace the magic of the stage, and embark on a theatrical journey that will bring fulfillment, friendships, and a sense of purpose to your retirement years.

2

11-20 Amazing Things to do in Retirement

1. Taking cooking classes and mastering new recipes can be a fun
    and delicious way to spend your retirement years. It allows you to
    expand your culinary skills, learn different cooking techniques,
    and explore diverse cuisines from around the world. Cooking
    classes offer the opportunity to connect with fellow food
    enthusiasts, share experiences, and experiment with new
    ingredients and flavors. Whether you aspire to become a gourmet
    chef or simply enjoy preparing meals for family and friends,
    cooking classes can be a delightful and rewarding hobby in
    retirement.

2. Starting a blog or writing a book about your life experiences
    offers a creative outlet and a chance to share your stories and
    wisdom with others. Retirement provides the perfect opportunity
    to reflect on your journey, document memories, and impart
    valuable lessons learned throughout your life. Blogging allows
    you to connect with a global audience, share your passions, and
    engage in meaningful discussions. Writing a book offers a
    tangible legacy that can be passed down to future generations
    and provides a sense of accomplishment and self-expression. It's
    a fun and introspective activity that allows you to reflect on your
    life and create something truly meaningful.

3. Learning to meditate and practicing mindfulness can bring a
    sense of calm, balance, and well-being to your retirement years.
    Meditation offers a tool to quiet the mind, reduce stress, and
    cultivate a sense of inner peace. By practicing mindfulness, you
    can enhance your ability to be present in the moment, appreciate
    life's simple pleasures, and develop a greater sense of self-
    awareness. Retirement provides the time and space to prioritize
    self-care and invest in practices that nurture your mental and
    emotional well-being.

4. Taking up birdwatching and exploring nature is a wonderful way to reconnect with the natural world and appreciate the beauty of wildlife. Birdwatching allows you to observe and identify different bird species, learn about their behaviors, and gain a deeper understanding of ecosystems and biodiversity. It offers opportunities to explore local parks, nature reserves, or even embark on birdwatching trips to different regions. Engaging with nature in retirement provides a sense of tranquility, an opportunity for physical activity, and a chance to marvel at the wonders of the natural world.

5. Starting a small business or consulting in your area of expertise can be an exciting and fulfilling venture in retirement. It allows you to leverage your skills, experience, and passion in a new and entrepreneurial way. Starting a small business offers opportunities for creativity, independence, and financial rewards. You can turn a hobby or a specialized knowledge into a profitable venture, whether it's opening a boutique shop, offering consulting services, or launching an online store. Retirement provides the freedom and flexibility to pursue your entrepreneurial dreams and explore new possibilities in the professional realm.

6. Attending concerts and live performances is a fantastic way to enjoy the magic of music, theater, or dance in retirement. Whether it's a local band performing at a nearby venue or a world-renowned orchestra in a grand concert hall, live performances offer a unique and immersive experience. The energy, talent, and creativity displayed by the artists can be inspiring and uplifting. Attending concerts allows you to appreciate different genres of music, discover new artists, and create cherished memories filled with the joy of live entertainment.

7. Joining a sports league or taking up a new sport is an excellent way to stay active, connect with others, and embrace a healthy lifestyle in retirement. Whether it's joining a local recreational soccer team, participating in a golf league, or trying out a new sport like pickleball or tennis, sports provide opportunities for physical fitness, friendly competition, and social engagement.

Being part of a sports league allows you to build camaraderie with teammates, enjoy the thrill of teamwork, and maintain a regular exercise routine that promotes overall well-being.

8. Organizing a regular game night with friends is a fun and social activity that can bring laughter, friendly competition, and cherished moments. Gather a group of friends, choose a variety of board games, card games, or even trivia games, and enjoy an evening of entertainment and friendly banter. Game nights provide an opportunity to connect with friends on a regular basis, strengthen relationships, and create lasting memories filled with joy and shared experiences.

9. Learning to play chess or other strategic games is an engaging and intellectually stimulating pursuit in retirement. Chess, in particular, challenges strategic thinking, problem-solving, and concentration. It offers an opportunity to exercise your mind, develop analytical skills, and engage in friendly competition with fellow chess enthusiasts. Strategic games like chess provide a mental workout, promote cognitive agility, and offer a lifelong pursuit of improvement and mastery.

10. Taking up fishing or boating as a hobby allows you to connect with nature, relax, and enjoy the serenity of the water. Fishing offers a peaceful and contemplative activity that allows you to spend time in natural surroundings, whether it's on a tranquil lake, river, or even by the ocean. It provides an opportunity to unwind, appreciate the beauty of the outdoors, and challenge yourself as you develop fishing skills and techniques. Boating, on the other hand, offers a chance to explore waterways, engage in recreational activities like water skiing or sailing, and enjoy leisurely cruises with family and friends. Fishing and boating as hobbies offer a sense of freedom, connection to nature, and an escape from the hustle and bustle of everyday life.

In conclusion, attending concerts, joining sports leagues, organizing game nights, learning strategic games, and taking up fishing or boating are all exciting and enjoyable activities to pursue in retirement. They provide opportunities for entertainment, social connection, physical activity, intellectual stimulation, and connection with the natural world. These activities can enrich your retirement years, foster a sense of fulfillment, and create lasting memories filled with fun and joy. So, embrace these activities, explore new interests, and make the most of your retirement by engaging in activities that bring you happiness and fulfillment.

3

21-30 Activities to do in Retirement

1. Exploring hiking trails and going on nature walks is an excellent way to stay active, connect with the outdoors, and appreciate the beauty of the natural world in retirement. Hiking allows you to explore scenic landscapes, encounter diverse flora and fauna, and experience the serenity of nature. It offers opportunities for physical exercise, fresh air, and a chance to disconnect from daily stresses. Exploring hiking trails and going on nature walks can be a source of adventure, relaxation, and rejuvenation.

2. Starting a garden and growing your own vegetables can be a rewarding and fulfilling hobby in retirement. Gardening allows you to connect with nature, nurture living plants, and witness the fruits of your labor as you cultivate your own edible produce. It provides an opportunity to spend time outdoors, engage in physical activity, and develop new skills related to planting, pruning, and harvesting. Starting a garden allows you to enjoy the beauty of flowers, enjoy the taste of homegrown vegetables, and create a tranquil oasis right in your backyard.

3. Learning yoga or tai chi for relaxation and fitness is a wonderful way to promote physical and mental well-being in retirement. These practices combine gentle movements, breathwork, and mindfulness to improve flexibility, strength, and overall balance. Yoga and tai chi provide a holistic approach to fitness, promoting relaxation, stress reduction, and cultivating a sense of inner calm. Participating in yoga or tai chi classes allows you to connect with others, learn from experienced instructors, and create a routine that fosters self-care and wellness.

4. Joining a local choir or singing group offers a fun and fulfilling activity for those with a passion for music and singing. Choirs and singing groups provide opportunities to engage in group performances, harmonize with others, and share the joy of music

with audiences. Joining a choir allows you to develop your vocal skills, learn new repertoire, and connect with fellow music enthusiasts. Singing has numerous health benefits, including stress reduction, increased lung capacity, and a boost in mood. Being part of a choir or singing group can bring a sense of camaraderie, self-expression, and the opportunity to create beautiful music together.

5. Taking up woodworking or DIY projects is a hands-on and creative hobby that allows you to engage in crafting and building with your own hands. Woodworking offers the opportunity to create functional or decorative items using various tools and techniques. It allows you to explore your creativity, learn new skills, and produce unique pieces of furniture, artwork, or home decor. Engaging in DIY projects allows you to personalize your living space, repurpose materials, and tackle projects that reflect your interests and needs. Woodworking and DIY projects offer a sense of accomplishment, a chance to work with different materials, and the satisfaction of creating something tangible.

6. Learning to knit, crochet, or quilt can be a delightful and creative hobby in retirement. These activities offer opportunities to express your artistic side, create beautiful handmade items, and engage in a calming and meditative process. Knitting, crocheting, or quilting allows you to work with different textures, colors, and patterns, unleashing your creativity and producing unique pieces. These crafts can provide a sense of accomplishment, as you create functional or decorative items that can be cherished or shared with others.

7. Becoming a mentor to young professionals in your field allows you to share your knowledge, expertise, and experiences acquired throughout your career. Mentoring offers the opportunity to give back to the next generation, guide others in their professional development, and provide valuable insights and support. Sharing your wisdom and offering guidance can be a rewarding and fulfilling way to make a positive impact, contribute to the growth of others, and create meaningful connections.

8. Attending workshops and seminars on topics that interest you is a wonderful way to continue learning and expand your

knowledge in retirement. Workshops and seminars offer opportunities to delve deeper into subjects you are passionate about or explore new areas of interest. Whether it's attending a lecture on history, participating in a cooking demonstration, or learning about new technologies, these events provide intellectual stimulation, engage your curiosity, and foster personal growth. They also offer the chance to connect with like-minded individuals and build a community around shared interests.

9. Joining a writing group and sharing your stories is a creative and enriching activity that allows you to explore your writing skills and connect with fellow writers. Writing groups provide a supportive and collaborative environment where you can share your work, receive feedback, and engage in constructive discussions. Joining a writing group offers opportunities for personal expression, skill development, and the chance to create written pieces that can be shared with others. It can be a platform for storytelling, memoir writing, or even exploring fiction and poetry.

10. Exploring genealogy and tracing your family history can be a fascinating and meaningful endeavor in retirement. Genealogy allows you to uncover your ancestral roots, discover stories about your family's past, and connect with relatives near and far. It offers an opportunity to dive into historical records, interview family members, and explore online resources to piece together your family's heritage. Exploring genealogy can provide a sense of belonging, a connection to your heritage, and the chance to leave a legacy for future generations.

In conclusion, learning to knit, crochet, or quilt; becoming a mentor to young professionals; attending workshops and seminars; joining a writing group; and exploring genealogy offer a wide range of enjoyable and fulfilling activities in retirement. They provide opportunities for creativity, personal growth, intellectual stimulation, and connection with others. Engaging in these activities can bring joy, fulfillment, and a sense of purpose in your retirement years. So, embrace these opportunities, explore new interests, and make the most of your retirement by engaging in activities that inspire and bring you happiness.

4

31-40 Amusing Things to do in Retirement

1. Volunteering at a local animal shelter is a rewarding and heartwarming activity in retirement. It allows you to contribute to the well-being of animals in need, provide them with care and attention, and support the efforts of the shelter. Volunteering at an animal shelter offers opportunities to interact with a variety of animals, help with feeding and grooming, assist in adoption events, or even offer training and socialization. It provides a sense of purpose, compassion, and the joy of making a positive difference in the lives of animals.

2. Taking up golfing and enjoying the outdoors is a popular and enjoyable activity for many retirees. Golf offers opportunities to appreciate nature, engage in physical activity, and challenge yourself in a leisurely and scenic setting. Whether you're a beginner or an experienced golfer, golfing provides a chance to improve your skills, enjoy time with friends on the course, and experience the thrill of the game. It offers a healthy way to stay active, connect with others, and savor the beauty of well-manicured greens and lush landscapes.

3. Starting a collection of something you love is a fun and personalized hobby that allows you to indulge in your interests and passions. Collecting can range from items like stamps, coins, artwork, vintage cars, or even antiques. Building a collection offers opportunities for exploration, research, and acquiring unique pieces that hold personal value. It can be a lifelong pursuit, providing a sense of excitement, fulfillment, and the joy of curating a collection that reflects your interests and tastes.

4. Exploring different types of cuisine and trying new restaurants is a delightful way to expand your culinary horizons and enjoy new flavors and dining experiences. Retirement offers the time and flexibility to explore local restaurants, experiment with cooking,

or even embark on food adventures during travels. Trying different types of cuisine allows you to appreciate the diversity of culinary traditions, discover new ingredients and cooking techniques, and savor the delights of regional and international dishes. It can be a social and cultural activity that brings friends and family together to share memorable dining experiences.

5. Learning to paint or draw and expressing your creativity is a fulfilling and therapeutic activity in retirement. Painting or drawing offers a means of self-expression, allowing you to explore your artistic abilities, experiment with different mediums, and create visual representations of your imagination or the world around you. Whether you choose to paint landscapes, portraits, still life, or abstract art, the act of painting or drawing can be a source of relaxation, inspiration, and personal growth. It provides an outlet for creativity, a way to tell stories visually, and a chance to develop a new skill that brings joy and satisfaction.

6. Joining a hiking or cycling club offers the opportunity to stay active, connect with nature, and enjoy the company of like-minded individuals. Hiking and cycling clubs provide organized outings, group activities, and a supportive community of outdoor enthusiasts. By joining a club, you can explore new trails, discover scenic routes, and experience the joy of being in nature. These activities promote physical fitness, provide mental refreshment, and offer a chance to forge new friendships while enjoying the great outdoors.

7. Taking up astronomy and stargazing is a fascinating and awe-inspiring hobby that allows you to explore the wonders of the universe. Learning about astronomy opens up a whole new world of celestial bodies, constellations, and astronomical events. Stargazing offers an opportunity to appreciate the night sky, observe planets, stars, and other celestial phenomena. By delving into astronomy, you can expand your knowledge, invest in a telescope, and embark on nocturnal adventures that bring a sense of wonder and cosmic connection.

8. Learning to play poker or bridge and joining a card club can be a fun and social activity in retirement. Card games provide

opportunities for mental stimulation, strategic thinking, and friendly competition. Joining a card club offers the chance to meet new people, engage in regular game nights, and improve your card-playing skills. These activities promote camaraderie, provide an outlet for friendly banter, and offer the excitement of games that require skill, strategy, and a bit of luck.

9. Starting a fitness routine and staying active is crucial for maintaining physical health and well-being in retirement. Engaging in regular exercise can improve cardiovascular health, enhance strength and flexibility, and boost overall energy levels. Retirement offers the flexibility to explore various fitness activities such as swimming, yoga, dancing, or strength training. Establishing a fitness routine not only improves physical health but also promotes mental well-being, increases longevity, and provides a sense of accomplishment and vitality in daily life.

10. Joining a photography club and sharing your work allows you to explore your creativity, connect with fellow photography enthusiasts, and showcase your talents. Photography clubs offer a platform to exchange ideas, receive feedback, and learn from others. By joining a club, you can participate in group outings, photo contests, and exhibitions, fostering a sense of community and appreciation for the art of photography. Sharing your work allows you to tell visual stories, evoke emotions, and leave a lasting impact on others.

In conclusion, joining a hiking or cycling club, taking up astronomy and stargazing, learning to play poker or bridge, starting a fitness routine, and joining a photography club are all enjoyable and enriching activities in retirement. They offer opportunities for staying active, connecting with nature, engaging in mental stimulation, promoting social interaction, and exploring artistic expression. Engaging in these activities can bring joy, fulfillment, and a sense of purpose in your retirement years. So, embrace these opportunities, pursue your passions, and make the most of your retirement by engaging in activities that inspire and bring you happiness.

5

Conclusion

In conclusion, retirement offers a multitude of opportunities for engaging in fun and fulfilling activities that cater to your interests, passions, and personal growth. Whether you choose to explore the great outdoors, embrace creative pursuits, connect with communities, or embark on new adventures, retirement provides the time and freedom to make the most of these experiences. Engaging in these activities not only brings joy and fulfillment but also promotes physical, mental, and emotional well-being.

By participating in hobbies and activities, you can expand your knowledge, develop new skills, and stay intellectually engaged. These pursuits allow you to connect with like-minded individuals, build friendships, and foster a sense of community. They offer opportunities for personal expression, creativity, and continuous learning, bringing a sense of purpose and satisfaction to your retirement years.

Retirement is a time to prioritize self-care and well-being. Engaging in physical activities, whether through sports, fitness routines, or outdoor adventures, promotes a healthy lifestyle and contributes to maintaining physical vitality. Taking time for relaxation, mindfulness practices, or artistic endeavors nurtures mental and emotional well-being, fostering a sense of balance and tranquility.

Furthermore, retirement provides a unique opportunity to give back and contribute to the greater community. Volunteering, mentoring, and engaging in philanthropic endeavors allow you to make a positive impact, share your expertise, and create meaningful connections with others. By dedicating your time and talents to causes that are close to your heart, you can leave a lasting legacy and create a sense of fulfillment through service.

Ultimately, the key to a fulfilling retirement lies in embracing the activities that bring you joy, ignite your passions, and align with your values. From pursuing creative arts, exploring nature, participating in social clubs, or engaging in personal growth, the possibilities are endless. So, seize the moment, embrace the opportunities, and make the most of your retirement by engaging in activities that inspire and bring you happiness. Your retirement years are yours to enjoy and savor, creating memories and experiences that will enrich your life for years to come.

Printed in Great Britain
by Amazon

35479953R00020